The Little
WOK
Cookbook

The Little
WOK
COOKBOOK

ULTIMATE
EDITIONS

First published by Ultimate Editions in 1996

© 1996 Anness Publishing Limited

Ultimate Editions is an imprint of
Anness Publishing Limited
1 Boundary Row
London SE1 8HP

This edition distributed in Canada by
Book Express, an imprint of
Raincoast Books Distribution Limited

ISBN 1 86035 183 2

Publisher Joanna Lorenz
Senior Cookery Editor Linda Fraser
Assistant Editor Emma Brown
Copy Editor Jenni Fleetwood
Designer Patrick McLeavey
Illustrator Anna Koska
Photographers Michelle Garrett, James Duncan, Edward Allwright &
Amanda Heywood
Recipes Liz Trigg, Catherine Atkinson, Deh-Ta Hsiung, Steven Wheeler &
Shirley Gill

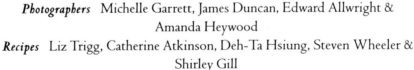

For all recipes, quantities are given in both metric and imperial measures, and, where
appropriate, measures are also given in standard cups and spoons. Follow one set, but not
a mixture, because they are not interchangeable.

Printed in China

Contents

Introduction

Where would we be without the wok? It is probably the single most useful pan in the kitchen. The deep bowl and angled sides make it ideal for stir-frying, steaming and braising. It can be used for soups, rice and noodle dishes, is handy for deep frying dumplings and can even be used to toss a hot salad.

Wok cookery is generally healthy. Stir-fries usually consist largely of vegetables, with a small amount of high quality protein, and the rapid cooking means that more nutrients are retained and fat-absorption is limited. Steamed foods lose a small amount of nutrients to the water, but this can be used as the basis for a soup.

Small wonder that the wok grows more popular by the day – and not simply for Chinese and Thai cooking. A number of the recipes in this collection, including Glazed Lamb and Stir-fried Duck with Blueberries, have no association with the orient, but nevertheless owe their superb flavour to speedy cooking in a wok.

For anyone whose kitchen facilities are limited, a wok is a real boon. You cook in it, serve from it, and it is easy to clean. Season a new wok properly and it will only need rinsing in hot water before being dried, oiled and put away.

Woks come in a range of materials, at prices to sort all pockets, singly or in boxed sets with accessories. For even heating and durability, the basic carbon steel wok – the sort you see in Chinese shops the world over – remains the best value. Pau woks (with one handle) are designed for stir-frying, while twin-handled Cantonese woks are preferred for steaming and deep frying.

Very few accessories are required. A couple of sharp knives – a small vegetable knife and a flat-bladed cook's knife – will be adequate for preparing ingredients, although those who have got to grips with the cleaver find this kitchen tool indispensable. Not only does it chop, dice, slice and crush (ginger and garlic) but the blade can be used to ferry the food to the wok.

It is convenient to have several chopping boards (some Chinese cooks use sections of tree trunk). For turning food when stir-frying, traditionalists use a long-handled forged iron ladle with a matching turner (shaped to the curve of the wok), but a couple of wooden spoons, or a spoon and spatula, can be used instead. A skimmer is handy, but you can substitute a slotted spoon.

Improvisation is the name of the game when it comes to wok cookery. If you like the look of a recipe, but haven't got the requisite ingredients, substitute. Just remember that colours, flavours and textures should be in balance.

Wok cookery is so rapid that every-thing must be ready before you begin. Mix marinades, measure out sauces and flavourings, and arrange all the ingredients in order of use. Having set the scene, relax and enjoy yourself. Wok cookery is great fun!

Ingredients

CHINESE EGG NOODLES

Available fresh and dried, these come in various widths and are sold in bundles. They take very little time to cook and may merely need a quick dip in boiling water before serving. Follow the instructions on the packet.

SESAME OIL

An aromatic oil used for adding flavour to foods towards the end of cooking. Sesame oil can be used for stir-frying but burns easily, so is best mixed with sunflower oil.

GRAPESEED OIL

With its delicate flavour, this light oil will not mask the taste of stir-fried ingredients.

RICE WINE

Made from fermented steamed white rice, this popular drink is widely used to flavour stir-fries. If unavailable, substitute dry sherry.

CHILLI SAUCE

This bottled sauce is a very hot blend of chillies, vinegar and salt. Use sparingly. For a milder flavour, use sweet chilli sauce.

BEAN SAUCE

Both yellow and black bean sauce are made from ground soya beans fermented with flour and salt. Black bean sauce has the stronger flavour and is widely used with seafood.

SOY SAUCE

Available in various strengths, light soy sauce has more flavour than the sweeter dark soy sauce. Japanese *shoyu* has a different, very distinctive taste.

OYSTER SAUCE

This savoury sauce is made from oyster flesh and juice, with water, sugar, salt and starch. It enhances the flavour of meat and vegetable dishes without making them taste fishy.

8

DRIED BLACK CHINESE MUSHROOMS AND FUNGI

Although these look rather uninteresting when dry, they plump up when soaked in water for 25–30 minutes and make a delicious addition to stir-fries. Discard the stem. Wood Ears and Cloud Ears are popular dried black fungi. When they are soaked in water they look gelatinous but taste crunchy.

BAMBOO SHOOTS

Young bamboo shoots have a delicate flavour. They are available canned, in large chunks or thin slices. Drain well before use.

LEMON GRASS

Fresh lemon grass has a wonderful citrus flavour. In stir-braises it is often used whole, in which case the stem is bruised and the grass then removed before serving. Alternatively, the lower part of the stem can be chopped or sliced before being stir-fried.

GINGER

Fresh ginger adds fragrance and flavour. Store it in the fridge (wrapped in polythene or peeled and sliced in sherry) or freeze it. Frozen ginger grates very easily and does not need peeling.

9

CORIANDER

This leafy green herb is a very common accompaniment to oriental meat and fish dishes. It is sometimes called Chinese parsley, cilantro or Greek parsley. It has an intensely aromatic flavour.

BEAN CURD

Also known as tofu, this is made from processed soya beans and is highly nutritious. Various forms are available, from a light creamy tofu (ideal for dips or desserts) to a firm type, which may be plain, flavoured or smoked. Firm tofu is ideal for stir-frying as it retains its shape when cooked.

Techniques

SEASONING THE WOK

Seasoning, in this instance, has nothing to do with salt and pepper. It's a technique for preparing a new utensil for use, so that ingredients do not stick in the future. Wash and dry the wok thoroughly. Pour a little oil into the wok and spread it around to coat the inside thoroughly, using a wad of kitchen paper. Keep rubbing the surface until the paper comes away clean. Place the pan over a high heat until very hot, then cool.

CLEANING THE WOK

Rinse the wok with hot water, scrub lightly with a bamboo brush or non-abrasive pad and dry thoroughly with kitchen paper or over a moderate heat. To prevent rust, coat the wok lightly with oil before storing.

PREPARING INGREDIENTS

So that food cooks quickly and evenly, cut it into small pieces of uniform size. Slice meats, leaf vegetables and mushrooms across the grain; celery and spring onions diagonally. Alternatively, cut vegetables into julienne strips (thin matchsticks).

SIMPLE STIR-FRYING

Start by heating a clean, dry wok. When it is hot, drizzle a "necklace" of oil all around the inner rim, give it a few seconds to coat the wok and heat through, then add the ingredients in order, with those that require longest cooking first. Using a ladle and turner or two wooden spoons, toss all the ingredients over the heat as when mixing a salad. Add seasonings at the end of cooking.

BAO

This is a method of rapid stir-frying which takes its name from a Chinese word meaning "to explode". The food is cooked very quickly over intense heat, so any ingredients that are likely to need longer cooking are par-boiled or steamed in advance. Marinades and sauces are sometimes used.

STIR-BRAISING

In this method of cooking, the principal ingredient, such as meat or poultry, is cooked first, then removed from the wok while vegetables and aromatics are stir-fried. All the ingredients are then brought together with sauces and stock, thickened with cornflour and rapidly braised before serving.

DEEP FRYING

The best style of wok for deep frying is the Cantonese twin-handled type, with a deep bowl. It is essential that the wok is completely stable: unless the wok is flat-bottomed you may need to use a stand. Do not preheat the wok before adding the oil and fill to no more than half full. Add only a few items at a time, and never leave the wok unattended. Keep a lid nearby. Use a skimmer or a slotted spoon to remove cooked food.

STEAMING

Many wok sets come complete with steamer racks. You can also buy bamboo stacking steamers, which are very useful, as you can steam several foods simultaneously. Cover the top steamer with a bamboo lid or foil. Alternatively, improvise by using a metal trivet topped with a plate. Cover with the domed lid of the wok and steam the food until tender, topping up the water as required.

11

COOK'S TIP

To toss a hot salad: Stir-fry bacon with onion, celery and garlic in a little oil, then sweep these ingredients to the sides of the wok. Add just enough red wine vinegar and soy sauce to the oil and bacon fat to make a flavoursome dressing, then add the torn leaves of an Iceberg lettuce. Toss swiftly with the other ingredients and serve at once.

Starters

Sweetcorn & Chicken Soup

INGREDIENTS

1 chicken breast fillet, about 115g/4oz, cubed
10ml/2 tsp light soy sauce
15ml/1 tbsp Chinese rice wine
5ml/1 tsp cornflour
60ml/4 tbsp cold water
5ml/1 tsp sesame oil
30ml/2 tbsp groundnut oil
5ml/1 tsp grated fresh root ginger
1 litre/1¾ pints/4 cups chicken stock
425g/15oz can cream-style sweetcorn
225g/8oz can sweetcorn kernels
2 eggs, beaten
2-3 spring onions, green parts only, cut in
thin rounds
salt and ground black pepper

SERVES 4–6

1 Mince all the chicken roughly in a food processor. Transfer to a bowl and stir in the soy sauce, rice wine, cornflour, water, sesame oil and seasoning. Cover and leave for 15 minutes. Heat a wok, add the groundnut oil and stir-fry the ginger briefly.

2 Add the stock and all the sweetcorn to the wok. When almost boiling, stir about 90ml/6 tbsp of the hot liquid into the chicken mixture until it forms a smooth paste. Add this to the wok. Slowly bring to the boil, stirring constantly, then simmer for 2–3 minutes.

3 Pour in the beaten eggs in a slow steady stream, using a fork or chopsticks to stir the top of the soup in a figure-of-eight pattern. The egg should set in lacy strands. Serve immediately, with the spring onions sprinkled on top.

Spiced Scallops in their Shells

INGREDIENTS

8 scallops, shelled, plus the cupped side of
4 shells
2 slices fresh root ginger, shredded
½ garlic clove, shredded
2 spring onions, green parts only, shredded
salt and ground black pepper
SAUCE
1 garlic clove, crushed
15ml/1 tbsp grated fresh root ginger
2 spring onions, white parts only, chopped
1-2 fresh green chillies, seeded
and finely chopped
15ml/1 tbsp light soy sauce
15ml/1 tbsp dark soy sauce
10ml/2 tsp sesame oil

SERVES 4

1 Remove the dark beard-like fringe and tough muscle from the scallops.

2 Place two scallops in each shell. Season with a little salt and pepper, then scatter the ginger, garlic and spring onions on top. Place the shells in a bamboo  steamer and steam for about 6 minutes until the scallops look opaque (you may have to do this in batches if your steamer is a small one).

3 Make the sauce. Mix the crushed garlic, fresh ginger, spring onion, chillies, light soy sauce, dark soy sauce and sesame oil together and stir well, until thoroughly blended. Pour the sauce into a small serving bowl.

4 Lift each shell out of the bamboo steamer – take care not to spill any of the juices. Arrange them on a large plate with the sauce bowl in the centre. Serve.

14

Thai Fish Cakes

INGREDIENTS

450g/1lb white fish fillets, such as cod
or haddock
3 spring onions, sliced
30ml/2 tbsp chopped fresh coriander
30ml/2 tbsp Thai red curry paste
1 fresh green chilli, seeded and chopped
10ml/2 tsp grated lime rind
15ml/1 tbsp lime juice
30ml/2 tbsp groundnut oil
salt, to taste
crisp lettuce leaves, shredded spring onions,
fresh red chilli slices, coriander sprigs
and lime wedges, to serve

SERVES 4

1 Cut the fish into chunks, then place in a blender or food processor. Add the sliced spring onions, coriander, red curry paste, green chilli, lime rind and lime juice to the fish. Season with salt. Process until finely minced.

2 Divide the mixture into 16 pieces and shape each one into a small cake, 4cm/1½in across (flouring your hands lightly may help). Arrange all the fish cakes on a plate, cover with clear film and chill for 2 hours, until firm. Heat the wok over a fairly high heat until hot. Add the oil and swirl it around.

3 Fry the fish cakes, in batches for 6–8 minutes, turning them over only once, until evenly browned. Drain each batch on kitchen paper and keep hot while cooking the remainder. Serve on a bed of crisp lettuce leaves with shredded spring onions, red chilli slices, coriander sprigs and lime wedges.

Aubergine with Sesame Chicken

INGREDIENTS

175g/6oz skinless, boneless chicken breast
1 spring onion, green part only, finely chopped
15ml/1 tbsp dark soy sauce
15ml/1 tbsp Mirin or sweet sherry
2.5ml/½ tsp sesame oil
1.5ml/¼ tsp salt
4 small aubergines, about 10cm/4in long
15ml/1 tbsp sesame seeds
plain flour, for dusting
vegetable oil, for deep frying
cucumber and carrot shapes, to garnish
DIPPING SAUCE
60ml/4 tbsp dark soy sauce
60ml/4 tbsp Dashi or vegetable stock
45ml/3 tbsp Mirin or sweet sherry

SERVES 4

1 Make the stuffing. Mince the chicken finely in a food processor. Add the spring onion, soy sauce, Mirin or sherry, sesame oil and salt. Make four slits in each aubergine, keeping them joined at the stem. Spoon the stuffing into the slits.

2 Dip each stuffed aubergine in the sesame seeds, then dust in flour. Set the aubergines aside. Make the dipping sauce by mixing the soy sauce, Dashi or stock and Mirin or sherry in a shallow bowl.

3 Heat the vegetable oil in a wok to 196°C/ 385°F. Fry the aubergines, two at a time, for about 3–4 minutes. Lift out with a slotted spoon on to kitchen paper to drain. Serve the aubergines at once, garnished with a few of the cucumber and carrot shapes.

Crispy Vegetable Spring Rolls

INGREDIENTS

115g/ 4oz young leeks or spring onions
115g/ 4oz carrots
115g/ 4oz/ 1 cup bamboo shoots
115g/ 4oz/ 1 cup mushrooms
225g/ 8oz/ 2 cups fresh beansprouts
45-60ml/ 3-4 tbsp vegetable oil
5ml/ 1 tsp salt
5ml/ 1 tsp soft light brown sugar
15ml/ 1 tbsp light soy sauce
15ml/ 1 tbsp Chinese rice wine or dry sherry
20 frozen spring roll skins, thawed
20ml/ 4 tbsp cornflour mixed to a paste with
25ml/ 5 tbsp water
plain flour, for dusting
oil, for deep frying
dipping suace, such as soy sauce, to serve

MAKES 40 ROLLS

1 Cut all the vegetables into thin shreds, roughly the same size and shape as the beansprouts.

2 Heat the oil in a wok and stir-fry the vegetables for about 1 minute. Add the salt, sugar, soy sauce and wine or sherry and heat through, stirring for 1½–2 minutes. Remove and drain off the excess liquid, then leave to cool.

3 To make the spring rolls, cut each spring roll skin in half diagonally, then place 15ml/1 tbsp of the vegetable mixture one-third of the way up on the

spring roll skin, with the triangle pointing away from you. Lift the long lower edge over the filling and roll once to enclose the filling.

4 Fold in both ends and roll once more, then brush the upper edge with a little cornflour paste, and roll into a neat package. Dust a large plate with

flour and place the spring rolls on to it, flap-side down. Cover loosely and set aside until needed.

5 To cook, heat the oil in a wok until hot, then reduce the heat to low. Deep fry the spring rolls in batches (about 8–10 at a time) for 2–3 minutes, or until golden and crispy, then lift out and drain on kitchen paper. Serve the spring rolls hot with a dipping sauce, such as soy sauce.

Fish & Shellfish Dishes

Fragrant Swordfish with Ginger & Lemon Grass

INGREDIENTS

1 kaffir lime leaf
45ml/ 3 tbsp sea salt
75ml/ 5 tbsp soft light brown sugar
4 swordfish steaks, about 225g/ 8oz each
1 lemon grass stalk, sliced
2.5cm/ 1in fresh root ginger, cut in matchsticks
1 lime
15ml/ 1 tbsp grapeseed oil
1 large ripe avocado
salt and ground black pepper
lime slices, to garnish

SERVES 4

1 Bruise the lime leaf by crushing slightly, to release the flavour. Make a marinade by processing the sea salt, brown sugar and lime leaf together in a food processor, until thoroughly blended.

2 Place the sword-fish steaks in a bowl. Sprinkle all the marinade over them and add the lemon grass and ginger. Cover and leave to marinate for 3–4 hours.

3 Rinse off the marinade and pat dry with kitchen paper. Pare the rind from the lime. Remove any excess pith, then cut it into very thin strips.

4 Heat the wok, then add the oil. When hot, add the lime rind, then the steaks, and stir-fry for 3–4 minutes. Add the juice of the lime. Remove from the heat. Cut

the avocado in half, remove the stone and peel and slice thinly. Season the fish and serve with the avocado, garnished with lime slices.

Sweet-&-Sour Fish

INGREDIENTS

450g/1lb white fish fillets, skinned, boned and cubed
2.5ml/½ tsp Chinese five-spice powder
5ml/1 tsp light soy sauce
1 egg, lightly beaten
30-45ml/2-3 tbsp cornflour
groundnut oil, for deep frying
SAUCE
10ml/2 tsp cornflour
60ml/4 tbsp water
60ml/4 tbsp pineapple juice
45ml/3 tbsp Chinese rice vinegar
45ml/3 tbsp caster sugar
10ml/2 tsp light soy sauce
30ml/2 tbsp tomato ketchup
10ml/2 tsp Chinese rice wine or dry sherry
45ml/3 tbsp groundnut oil
1 garlic clove, crushed
15ml/1 tbsp chopped fresh root ginger
6 spring onions, sliced diagonally in 5cm/2in lengths
1 green pepper, seeded and cut in 2cm/¾in squares
115g/4oz fresh pineapple, cubed
salt and ground black pepper

SERVES 3–4

1 Put the fish in a bowl. Sprinkle over the five-spice powder and soy sauce, then toss gently. Cover and leave to marinate for 30 minutes. Dip the fish in the

egg, then in the cornflour, coating it all over. Shake off any excess cornflour.

2 Half-fill a wok with oil and heat to 190°C/375°F. Deep fry the fish in batches for 2 minutes until golden. Drain and keep hot. Carefully pour away the oil and wipe the wok clean.

3 Make the sauce. Blend the cornflour, water, pineapple juice, rice vinegar, sugar, soy sauce, ketchup and rice wine or sherry together in a bowl. Mix well, then set aside.

4 Heat the wok until hot, add 30ml/2 tbsp of the oil and swirl it around. Add the garlic and ginger and stir-fry for a few seconds. Add the spring onions and green pepper squares and stir-fry over a medium heat for 2 minutes. Add the pineapple.

5 Stir in the cornflour mixture. Cook until thick. Stir in the remaining oil and add seasoning to taste. Pour the sauce over the fish and serve.

Ragoût of Shellfish with Sweet Scented Basil

INGREDIENTS

12 fresh mussels in their shells, scrubbed
60ml/ 4 tbsp water
400ml/ 14fl oz/ 1⅔ cups canned coconut milk
300ml/ ½ pint/ 1¼ cups chicken stock
225g/ 8oz prepared squid, cut in strips
350g/ 12oz monkfish or hokey, skinned
150g/ 5oz cooked prawns, peeled and deveined
4 scallops, sliced (optional)
50g/ 2oz/ ½ cup canned bamboo shoots, drained
75g/ 3oz/ ½ cup French beans, blanched
1 ripe tomato, peeled, seeded and roughly chopped
4 large leaf basil sprigs, torn, to garnish
boiled rice and chilli sauce, to serve
GREEN CURRY PASTE
10ml/ 2 tsp coriander seeds
2.5ml/ ½ tsp caraway or cumin seeds
3-4 medium green chillies, finely chopped
20ml/ 4 tsp caster sugar
10ml/ 2 tsp salt
1 piece lemon grass, 7.5cm/ 3in long
30ml/ 2 tbsp finely chopped fresh root ginger
3 garlic cloves
1 onion, finely chopped
1 piece shrimp paste, 2cm/ ¾in square
50g/ 2oz/ 1 cup coriander leaves, finely chopped
45ml/ 3 tbsp finely chopped fresh basil leaves
30ml/ 2 tbsp vegetable oil

SERVES 4–6

1 Put the mussels in a large saucepan, add the water, cover and cook for 6–8 minutes, until the mussels open (discard any that remain closed). Take two-thirds of them out of their shells. Set all the mussels aside, with the strained cooking liquid.

2 Make the curry paste. Dry-fry all the seeds in a wok to release their flavour. Grind the chillies to a smooth paste with the sugar and salt. Add the seeds, lemon grass, ginger, garlic and onion, and grind until smooth. Stir in the shrimp paste, herbs and vegetable oil.

3 Strain the coconut milk into a wok, reserving the solids in the strainer. Add the stock and about 60ml/4 tbsp of the green curry paste to the wok (keep the remaining paste in a covered jar in the fridge, for another occasion). Boil rapidly until the liquid has reduced by half.

4 Stir in all the squid, fish and coconut solids, then simmer for 15–20 minutes. Add the shellfish, bamboo shoots, beans, and tomato and simmer for  2–3 minutes. Season, then serve, garnished with basil, accompanied by boiled rice and chilli sauce.

Quick-fried Prawns with Hot Spices

INGREDIENTS

450g/1lb large raw prawns
2.5cm/1in fresh root ginger, grated
2 garlic cloves, crushed
5ml/1 tsp hot chilli powder
5ml/1 tsp ground turmeric
10ml/2 tsp black mustard seeds
seeds from 4 green cardamom pods, crushed
50g/2oz/4 tbsp ghee or butter
120ml/4fl oz/½ cup coconut milk
salt and ground black pepper
chopped fresh coriander, to garnish
naan bread, to serve

SERVES 2–4

1 Peel the prawns carefully, leaving the tails attached. Using a small sharp knife, make a slit along the back of each prawn and remove the dark vein. Rinse all the prawns under cold running water, drain and pat dry with kitchen paper.

2 Put the ginger, garlic, chilli powder, turmeric, mustard seeds and cardamom seeds in a bowl. Add the prawns and toss to coat with the spice mixture.

3 Heat a wok until hot. Add the ghee or butter and swirl it around until foaming.

4 Add the spiced prawns. Stir-fry them for about 1–1½ minutes until they are just turning pink. Stir in all the coconut milk and simmer for 3–4 minutes until the prawns are cooked. Season with salt and pepper, then sprinkle over the coriander, to garnish. Serve at once with naan bread.

26

Squid with Peppers in a Black Bean Sauce

INGREDIENTS

30ml/2 tbsp salted black beans
30ml/2 tbsp medium-dry sherry
15ml/1 tbsp light soy sauce
5ml/1 tsp cornflour
2.5ml/½ tsp caster sugar
30ml/2 tbsp water
45ml/3 tbsp groundnut oil
450g/1lb prepared squid, scored and cut in
thick strips
5ml/1 tsp finely chopped fresh root ginger
1 garlic clove, finely chopped
1 fresh green chilli, seeded and sliced
6-8 spring onions, cut diagonally in
short lengths
½ red and ½ green pepper, cored, seeded and
cut in 2.5cm/1in diamonds
75g/3oz/¾ cup shiitake mushrooms,
thickly sliced

SERVES 4

1 Rinse the black beans thoroughly and finely chop them. Place them in a bowl with the sherry, soy sauce, cornflour, sugar and water; mix well.

2 Heat a wok, add the oil, then stir-fry the squid briefly, until opaque. Remove with a slotted spoon.

3 Add the ginger, garlic and chilli to the wok. Stir-fry briefly, then add the vegetables and stir-fry for 2 minutes. Toss in the squid and the black bean sauce.

Cook, stirring, for about 1 minute or until thickened. Serve the stir-fry at once.

Poultry Dishes

Stir-fried Duck with Blueberries

INGREDIENTS

2 duck breasts, about 175g/6oz each
30ml/2 tbsp sunflower oil
15ml/1 tbsp red wine vinegar
5ml/1 tsp sugar
5ml/1 tsp red wine
5ml/1 tsp crème de cassis
115g/4oz/1 cup fresh blueberries
15ml/1 tbsp chopped fresh mint
salt and ground black pepper
fresh mint sprigs, to garnish
sliced celery and spring onion salad, to serve

SERVES 4 ·

2 Stir in all the fresh blueberries. Gently heat through, then sprinkle the mint over the top. Serve at once, garnished with mint sprigs, with the celery and spring onion salad.

1 With a cleaver or a sharp cook's knife, cut both duck breasts in neat thin slices. Season the duck generously, then heat the wok and add the oil. When the oil is hot, stir-fry the duck slices for 3 minutes. Add the red wine vinegar, sugar, red wine and crème de cassis. Boil for about 3 minutes, to reduce the liquid to a thick syrup.

29

Turkey with Sage, Prunes & Brandy

INGREDIENTS

115g / 4oz / ½ cup prunes
1.5kg / 3–3½ lb turkey breast
15ml / 1 tbsp fresh sage, chopped
300ml / ½ pint / 1¼ cups cognac or brandy
150g / 5oz smoked bacon, in one piece
50g / 2oz / 4 tbsp butter
24 baby onions, peeled and quartered
salt and ground black pepper
fresh sage sprigs, to garnish

SERVES 4

1 Stone the prunes and cut them into slivers. Remove the skin from the turkey and cut the breast into thin pieces.

2 Mix together all the prunes, sage, turkey, and cognac or brandy in a non-metallic dish. Cover and leave to marinate for 6–8 hours, or overnight in the fridge.

3 Strain the turkey and prunes, reserving the cognac mixture, and pat dry on kitchen paper.

4 Cut the smoked bacon into lardons (dice), place them on a plate and set aside. Heat the wok and add half the butter. When melted, add the baby onion quarters and stir-fry for about 4 minutes, until they are crisp and golden brown. Set aside.

5 Heat the wok, and stir-fry the bacon lardons for 1 minute. Stir until they release some fat. Add the remaining butter and stir-fry the turkey for about 3–4 minutes, until crisp and golden. Add the prunes and stir-fry briefly. Push the turkey mixture to one side in the wok and add the cognac mixture; simmer until thickened. Stir the turkey into the sauce, season well with salt and ground black pepper, and serve the stir-fry at once, garnished with sprigs of fresh sage.

Glazed Chicken with Cashew Nuts

INGREDIENTS

75g/3oz/¾ cup cashew nuts
45ml/3 tbsp groundnut oil
4 garlic cloves, finely chopped
1 red pepper, halved, seeded and sliced
in strips
450g/1lb skinless, boneless chicken breasts, cut
in strips
30ml/2 tbsp Chinese rice wine or medium-
dry sherry
45ml/3 tbsp hoi-sin sauce
10ml/2 tsp sesame oil
5-6 spring onions, green parts only, sliced
soy sauce, to serve

SERVES 4

2 Heat the wok again until hot, add the oil and swirl it around. Add the garlic and let it sizzle for a few seconds. Add the red pepper and chicken strips and stir-fry over a fairly high heat for 2 minutes. Do not let the garlic scorch or it will taste bitter.

3 Pour the rice wine or sherry and the hoi-sin sauce over the chicken mixture and mix well. Continue to stir-fry until the chicken is tender and evenly glazed.

1 Heat the wok until hot, then add the cashew nuts and stir-fry over a low to medium heat for 1–2 minutes, or until golden brown. Remove and set aside.

4 Stir in the sesame oil, then sprinkle all the cashew nuts and spring onions over the stir-fry. Toss quickly to mix, then serve with soy sauce.

Spicy Clay-pot Chicken

INGREDIENTS

1.5kg/ 3-3 ½lb chicken
45ml/ 3 tbsp freshly-grated coconut
30ml/ 2 tbsp vegetable oil
1 small onion, finely chopped
2 garlic cloves, crushed
1 piece galingal or fresh ginger, 2.5cm/ 1in
long, peeled and thinly sliced
2 small green chillies, seeded and finely chopped
15ml/ 1 tbsp fish sauce or 1 piece shrimp paste,
1cm/ ½in square
1 piece lemon grass, 5cm/ 2in long
400g/ 14fl oz/ 1⅔ cups canned coconut milk
300ml/ ½ pint/ 1¼ cups chicken stock
2 lime leaves (optional)
15ml/ 1 tbsp sugar
15ml/ 1 tbsp rice or white wine vinegar
2 ripe tomatoes, to garnish
30ml/ 2 tbsp chopped coriander leaves,
to garnish
boiled rice, to serve

SERVES 6

1 To joint the chicken, remove the legs and wings with a chopping knife. Skin the pieces and divide the drumsticks from the thighs. Using a pair of kitchen scissors, cut the breast from the carcass and cut it into four pieces. Set the chicken aside.

2 Dry-fry all the coconut in a large wok until evenly brown. Add the vegetable oil with the onion, garlic, galingal or ginger, chillies, the fish sauce or shrimp paste and lemon grass. Fry briefly over a moderate to high heat to release all the flavours.

3 Preheat the oven to 180°C/ 350°F /Gas 4. Add the chicken joints to the wok and brown evenly with the spices for 2–3 minutes.

4 Strain the coconut milk and add the thin part to the wok with the chicken stock, lime leaves if using, sugar and vinegar. Stir well and bring to the boil. Transfer to a glazed clay pot or casserole, cover and bake for 50–55 minutes, or until the chicken is tender. Stir in the thick part of the coconut milk and return to the oven for about 5–10 minutes to simmer and thicken.

5 Place the tomatoes in a bowl and cover with boiling water to loosen and remove the skins. Halve the tomatoes, remove the seeds and cut into large dice. Add the tomatoes to the finished dish, scatter with the chopped coriander and serve at once, with a large bowl of boiled rice.

Meat Dishes

Glazed Lamb

INGREDIENTS

15ml/1 tbsp grapeseed oil
450g/1lb boneless lean lamb, cut in thin
neat strips
175g/6oz mange-touts, topped and tailed
3 spring onions, sliced
30ml/2 tbsp clear honey
juice of ½ lemon
30ml/2 tbsp chopped fresh coriander, plus
extra sprigs to garnish
15ml/1 tbsp sesame seeds
salt and ground black pepper
lemon wedges, to serve

SERVES 4

2 Add the mange-touts and spring onions to the hot wok and stir-fry for about 30 seconds.

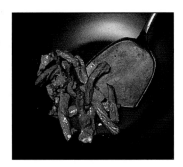

1 Heat the wok, then add the oil. When the oil is hot, stir-fry the lamb strips until browned all over. Remove the lamb from the wok and keep it hot.

3 Return the lamb to the wok and add the honey, lemon juice, the coriander and sesame seeds. Season and stir-fry briefly. Serve with lemon wedges, garnished with herbs.

Stir-fried Lamb with Spring Onions

INGREDIENTS

350-400g/12-14oz leg of lamb fillet,
thinly sliced
5ml/1 tsp soft light brown sugar
15ml/1 tbsp light soy sauce
15ml/1 tbsp Chinese rice wine or dry sherry
10ml/2 tsp cornflour, mixed to a paste with
15ml/1 tbsp water
15g/½oz dried black fungus (wood-ears)
about 60ml/4 tbsp vegetable oil
6-8 spring onions, thickly sliced
a few small pieces fresh root ginger
30ml/2 tbsp yellow bean sauce
a few drops sesame oil

SERVES 4

1 Marinate the lamb with the sugar, soy sauce, wine or sherry and cornflour paste for 30–45 minutes. Soak the fungus in water for 25–30 minutes, then cut into small pieces.

2 Heat the oil in a large wok until hot and stir-fry the meat for about 2–3 minutes, or until the colour changes. Remove with a slotted spoon and drain.

3 Keep about 15ml/ 1 tbsp of oil in the wok, then add all the spring onions, the ginger, fungus and yellow bean sauce. Blend well, then add the meat and stir-fry for about 1 minute. Sprinkle the sesame oil over the top, toss to mix, and serve at once.

Stir-fried Pork with Vegetables

INGREDIENTS

225g/8oz pork fillet, thinly sliced
15ml/1 tbsp light soy sauce, plus extra to taste
5ml/1 tsp soft light brown sugar
5ml/1 tsp Chinese rice wine or dry sherry
10ml/2 tsp cornflour, mixed to a paste with
15ml/1 tbsp water
60ml/4 tbsp vegetable oil
115g/4oz/1 cup mange-touts, topped
and tailed
115g/4oz/1 cup button mushrooms,
thinly sliced
1 medium or 2 small carrots, thinly sliced
1 spring onion, sliced
5ml/1 tsp salt
chicken stock or water, if necessary
a few drops sesame oil

SERVES 4

1 Marinate the pork with the soy sauce, sugar, wine or sherry and the cornflour paste.

2 Heat the oil in a preheated wok and stir-fry the pork for 2–3 minutes, or until its colour changes. Remove and keep warm

3 Stir-fry all the vegetables together for 2 minutes, then add the salt and pork, with a little stock or water, if necessary. Stir-fry for 1 minute more, then season with soy sauce, to taste. Sprinkle the sesame oil over the top and serve immediately.

39

Stir-fried Pork with Mustard

INGREDIENTS

40g/ 1½oz/ 3 tbsp unsalted butter
1 cooking apple, peeled, cored and thinly sliced
15ml/ 1 tbsp caster sugar
500g/ 1¼lb pork fillet, cut in thin slices
1 small onion, finely chopped
30ml/ 2 tbsp Calvados or other brandy
15ml/ 1 tbsp Meaux or coarse-grain mustard
150ml/ ¼ pint/ ⅔ cup double cream
30ml/ 2 tbsp chopped fresh parsley
flat-leaf parsley sprigs, to garnish

SERVES 4

2 Heat the wok, then add all the remaining butter and stir-fry the pork fillet and onion together for 2–3 minutes, until the pork is golden and onion tender.

3 Stir in the Calvados or other brandy and boil until it is reduced by half. Stir in the mustard.

4 Add the cream, stir to mix well, and simmer for about 1 minute. Add the chopped parsley. Stir, then serve, with a few sprigs of parsley, to garnish.

1 Heat the wok, then add half the butter. When the butter is hot, add the apple slices, sprinkle over the sugar, and stir-fry for 2–3 minutes. Remove the apple slices and set them aside. Wipe out the wok with kitchen paper and return it to the hob.

COOK'S TIP

Use bamboo chopsticks as Chinese cooks do: for moving food around in the wok; for beating egg or for lifting deep-fried items.

Sukiyaki-style Beef

INGREDIENTS

200g/ 7oz Japanese rice noodles
15ml/ 1 tbsp shredded suet
450g/ 1lb thick rump steak, thinly sliced
200g/ 7oz hard tofu, cut in cubes
8 shiitake mushrooms, trimmed
2 leeks, sliced in 2.5cm/ 1in lengths
salt
90g/ 3½oz/ 3 cups baby spinach
leaves, to serve
STOCK
15ml/ 1 tbsp caster sugar
90ml/ 6 tbsp rice wine
45ml/ 3 tbsp dark soy sauce
120ml/ 4fl oz/ ½ cup water

SERVES 4

1 Bring a saucepan of lightly salted water to the boil. Add the noddles and blanch for 2 minutes. Drain well. Mix all the stock ingredients in a bowl.

2 Heat the wok, then add the suet. Leave it to melt, then add the beef and stir-fry for 2–3 minutes. It should be cooked but still fairly pink in colour.

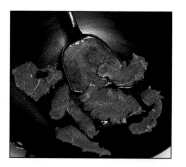

3 Pour the stock over the beef. Add the rest of the ingredients. Cook for 4 minutes or until the leeks are tender. Serve a selection of all the ingredients to each person, with a few baby spinach leaves. It is not necessary to add a garnish.

42

Beef with Cantonese Oyster Sauce

INGREDIENTS

275-350g/10-12oz beef steak, thinly sliced
5ml/1 tsp soft light brown sugar
15ml/1 tbsp light soy sauce
10ml/2 tsp Chinese rice wine or dry sherry
10ml/2 tsp cornflour, mixed to a paste with
15ml/1 tbsp water
60ml/4 tbsp vegetable oil
1 spring onion, sliced
a few small pieces fresh root ginger
115g/4oz/1 cup mange-touts, topped
and tailed
115g/4oz/1 cup baby corn cobs, halved
115g/4oz/1 cup drained canned
straw mushrooms
2.5ml/½ tsp salt
30ml/2 tbsp oyster sauce

SERVES 4

1 In a bowl, marinate the beef with the sugar, soy sauce, rice wine or sherry and cornflour paste for 25–30 minutes, stirring the mixture occasionally.

2 Heat the oil in a large wok and fry the beef for 2–3 minutes, until the colour changes. Remove the beef with a slotted spoon and drain.

3 Pour off the excess oil, leaving 30ml/2 tbsp in the wok, add the spring onion, ginger, the vegetables and salt. Stir-fry for 2–3 minutes, then return the

beef slices to the wok. Add the oyster sauce. Blend well and serve immediately.

44

Stir-fried Beef & Broccoli

INGREDIENTS

350g/12oz rump steak
15ml/1 tbsp cornflour
5ml/1 tsp sesame oil
350g/12oz broccoli, cut in small florets
4 spring onions, sliced diagonally
1 carrot, cut in matchstick strips
1 garlic clove, crushed
2.5cm/1in fresh root ginger, cut in very fine strips
120ml/4fl oz/½ cup beef stock
30ml/2 tbsp soy sauce
30ml/2 tbsp dry sherry
10ml/2 tsp soft light brown sugar
spring onion tassels, to garnish
egg noodles or rice, to serve

SERVES 4

1 Trim the beef and cut into thin slices across the grain. Cut each slice into thin strips. Toss in the cornflour to coat thoroughly. Heat the sesame oil in a wok. Add the beef strips and stir-fry over a high heat for 3 minutes. Remove and set aside.

2 Add the broccoli, spring onions, carrot, garlic clove, ginger strips and beef stock to the wok. Cover and simmer for 3 minutes. Remove the lid and cook, stirring, until the stock has evaporated, leaving behind the flavoured vegetable mixture.

3 Mix the soy sauce, sherry and brown sugar together. Add the mixture to the wok, then add the beef. Cook for 2–3 minutes, stirring continuously. Spoon into a warm serving dish and garnish with spring onion tassels. Serve with egg noodles or rice.

Vegetable Dishes

Pok Choi & Mushroom Stir-fry

INGREDIENTS

4 dried black Chinese mushrooms
150ml/ ¼ pint/ ½ cup boiling water
15ml/ 1 tbsp vegetable oil
1 garlic clove, crushed
450g/ 1lb pok choi, torn in bite-size pieces
50g/ 2oz/ ½ cup oyster mushrooms, halved
if large
50g/ 2oz/ ½ cup shiitake mushrooms,
halved if large
30ml/ 2 tbsp oyster sauce

SERVES 4

1 Put the dried black mushrooms in a bowl. Pour over the boiling water and leave for about 15 minutes to soak and soften. Drain the mushrooms thoroughly.

2 Heat the wok, then add the oil. When the oil is hot, add the crushed garlic and stir-fry over a medium heat until softened but not coloured.

3 Add the pok choi and stir-fry for 1 minute. Mix in all the mushrooms and stir-fry for 1 minute.

4 Drizzle the oyster sauce over the mixture, toss well and serve immediately.

Stir-fried Vegetables with Coriander Omelette

INGREDIENTS

15ml/ 1 tbsp cornflour
30ml/ 2 tbsp soy sauce
15ml/ 1 tbsp sweet chilli sauce
120ml/ 4fl oz/ ½ cup vegetable stock
30ml/ 2 tbsp groundnut oil
5ml/ 1 tsp grated fresh root ginger
6-8 spring onions, sliced
115g/ 4oz/ 1 cup mange-touts
1 yellow pepper, seeded and sliced
*115g/ 4oz/ 1 cup fresh shiitake or
button mushrooms*
*75g/ 3oz/ ½ cup drained canned water
chestnuts, rinsed*
115g/ 4oz/ 2 cups beansprouts
½ small Chinese cabbage, coarsely shredded
OMELETTE
2 eggs
30ml/ 2 tbsp water
45ml/ 3 tbsp chopped fresh coriander
15ml/ 1 tbsp groundnut oil
salt and ground black pepper

SERVES 3–4

1 Make the omelette. Whisk the eggs, water, coriander and seasoning in a small bowl. Heat the oil in a wok. Pour in the eggs, then tilt the wok so that the mixture spreads to an even layer. Cook over a high heat until the edges are slightly crisp.

2 With a wok spatula or palette knife, flip the omelette over. Cook the other side for 30 seconds, until it is lightly browned. Turn the omelette on to a board and leave to cool. When cold, roll up loosely and cut across into thin slices. Set the omelette strands aside. Wipe the wok clean, using a pad of kitchen paper.

3 In a bowl, blend together the cornflour, soy sauce, chilli sauce and stock. Set aside.

4 Heat the wok until hot. Add the oil and swirl it around, add the ginger and spring onions and stir-fry for a few seconds to flavour the oil. Add the mange-touts, pepper, mushrooms and water chestnuts and stir-fry for 3 minutes over a fairly high heat.

5 Add the beansprouts and the coarsely shredded Chinese cabbage. Stir-fry for 2 minutes.

6 Pour in the cornflour mixture, stir to mix, then cook, stirring, for about 1 minute, until the glaze thickens and coats the vegetables. Turn all the vegetables on to a warmed serving plate and arrange the omelette strands on top. Serve at once.

48

Crispy "Seaweed" with Flaked Almonds

INGREDIENTS

450g/1lb spring greens
groundnut oil, for deep frying
1.5ml/¼ tsp sea salt flakes
5ml/1 tsp caster sugar
50g/2oz/½ cup flaked almonds, toasted

SERVES 4

1 Remove and discard the thick white stalks from the spring greens. Also discard discoloured leaves.

2 Lay several leaves on top of one another, roll up tightly and slice into thread-like strips.

3 Half-fill a deep wok with oil and heat to 180°C/350°F. Deep fry the spring greens in batches for about 1 minute, until they darken and become crisp. Remove each batch from the wok as soon as it is ready and drain on kitchen paper.

4 Transfer the "seaweed" to a serving dish, sprinkle with the salt and sugar, then mix well. Scatter over the toasted flaked almonds and serve.

50

Deep Fried Root Vegetables with Spiced Salt

INGREDIENTS

1 carrot, cut in long, thin ribbons
2 parsnips, cut in long, thin ribbons
2 raw beetroots, cut in thin rounds
1 sweet potato, cut in thin rounds
groundnut oil, for deep frying
1.5ml/¼ tsp chilli powder
5ml/1 tsp sea salt flakes

SERVES 4–6

51

1 Half-fill a wok with oil and heat to 180°C/350°F. Add the vegetable slices in batches and deep fry for 2–3 minutes, until crisp. Remove and drain well.

2 Place the chilli powder and sea salt in a mortar and grind together to a coarse powder.

3 Pile up the vegetable "crisps" on a serving plate and sprinkle over the spiced salt. Serve at once.

COOK'S TIP

To save time you can also slice the vegetables using a mandoline or food processor with a thin slicing disc attached. Other root vegetables also work well in this recipe.

Yu Hsiang Aubergine in Spicy Sauce

INGREDIENTS

3-4 whole dried red chillies, soaked in water
for 10 minutes
vegetable oil, for deep frying
450g/ 1lb aubergines, cut in short strips
1 garlic clove, finely chopped
5ml/ 1 tsp finely chopped fresh ginger
5ml/ 1 tsp finely chopped spring onion,
white part only
115g/ 4oz lean pork, thinly shredded
15ml/ 1 tbsp light soy sauce
5ml/ 1 tsp soft light brown sugar
15ml/ 1 tbsp chilli bean sauce
15ml/ 1 tbsp Chinese rice wine or dry sherry
15ml/ 1 tbsp rice vinegar
10ml/ 2 tsp cornflour, mixed to a paste with
15ml/ 1 tbsp water
a few drops sesame oil
5ml/ 1 tsp finely chopped spring onions, green
part only, to garnish

SERVES 4

52

1 Drain the soaked red chillies well, cut them into small pieces and discard the seeds.

2 Heat the oil in a wok and deep fry the aubergine strips for 3–4 minutes, or until limp. Remove and drain on kitchen paper.

3 Leave 15ml/ 1 tbsp oil in the wok. Add the garlic, ginger, spring onion and chillies. Stir well. Add the pork and stir-fry until it is cooked. Add all the seasonings. Bring

to the boil. Add the aubergines and braise for 40 seconds, then thicken with the cornflour paste. Add the spring onions. Sprinkle with the sesame oil. Serve.

Braised Chinese Vegetables

INGREDIENTS

7g/ ¼oz dried black fungus (wood-ears)
225g/ 8oz tofu, cut in 12 small pieces
45-60ml/ 3-4 tbsp vegetable oil
85g/ 3oz/ ¾ cup straw mushrooms, drained
and halved if large
85g/ 3oz/ ¾ cup sliced bamboo shoots, drained
50g/ 2oz/ ½ cup mange-touts, topped
and tailed
175g/ 6oz Chinese leaves, cut in small pieces
5ml/ 1 tsp salt
2.5ml/ ½ tsp soft light brown sugar
15ml/ 1 tbsp light soy sauce
a few drops sesame oil (optional)

SERVES 4

1 Put the black fungus in a bowl of cold water to soak for 20–25 minutes, then rinse and discard the hard stalks, if there are any.

2 Add the tofu to a pan of boiling water and leave for 2 minutes until hardened. Drain. Heat the oil in a wok. Stir-fry the tofu until it is golden brown.

3 Using a slotted spoon, remove the tofu from the wok and drain on kitchen paper. Transfer to a plate and keep hot while you cook the vegetables.

4 Reheat the oil in the wok, add all the vegetables and stir-fry for 1½ minutes. Return the tofu pieces, with the salt, sugar and soy sauce. Continue to stir-fry for 1 minute more, then cover and braise for 2–3 minutes. Sprinkle with the seasame oil, if using, spoon on to a platter and serve at once.

Mixed Roasted Vegetables

INGREDIENTS

1 large aubergine cut lengthways in segments
225g/ 8oz/ ¾ cup salt, for sprinkling
30ml/ 2 tbsp olive oil
25g/ 1oz Parmesan cheese, in one piece
2 red peppers, seeded and cut lengthways
in segments
1 yellow pepper, seeded and cut lengthways
in segments
2 plum tomatoes, cut lengthways in segments
30ml/ 2 tbsp fresh parsley, chopped
ground black pepper
parsley or coriander sprigs, to garnish

SERVES 4

3 Heat the wok. Add 5ml/ I tsp of the oil. When it is hot, add the Parmesan and stir-fry until golden brown. Remove from the wok and allow it to cool.

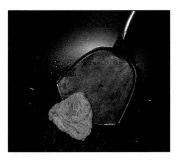

Place the Parmesan on a board and chop into fine flakes, using a cleaver or cook's knife.

4 Heat the wok, and then add the rest of the oil. When the oil is hot, stir-fry the aubergine and the peppers for 4–5 minutes. Stir in the tomatoes and

stir-fry for a further I minute. Toss the vegetables with the flaked Parmesan cheese and the chopped parsley. Add black pepper to taste. Transfer to a platter, garnish with sprigs of parsley or coriander and serve at once.

I Place all of the aubergine in a colander and then sprinkle with salt. Leave for about 30 minutes, to allow the salt to draw out all the bitter juices.

2 Rinse off the salt in cold water, then drain the aubergine well and pat dry on kitchen paper.

Rice & Noodle Dishes

Crispy Noodles with Mixed Vegetables

INGREDIENTS

groundnut oil, for deep frying
115g/4oz/1 cup dried vermicelli rice noodles,
broken in 7.5cm/3in lengths
115g/4oz/scant 1 cup runner beans, cut in
short lengths or French beans, trimmed
2.5cm/1in fresh root ginger, cut in shreds
1 fresh red chilli, seeded and sliced
175g/6oz/1½ cups fresh shiitake or button
mushrooms, thickly sliced
2 large carrots, cut in matchsticks
2 courgettes, cut in matchsticks
a few Chinese cabbage leaves, coarsely shredded
75g/3oz/1½ cups beansprouts
4 spring onions, shredded
30ml/2 tbsp light soy sauce
30ml/2 tbsp Chinese rice wine
5ml/1 tsp sugar
30ml/2 tbsp roughly torn coriander leaves

SERVES 3–4

1 Half-fill a deep wok with groundnut oil. Heat it to 180°C/350°F. Deep fry the raw noodles, a handful at a time, for 1–2 minutes until puffed and crispy. Drain on kitchen paper. Carefully pour off all but 30ml/2 tbsp of the oil. Reheat this, then add the beans and stir-fry for 2–3 minutes. Add the ginger shreds, chilli, mushrooms, carrots and courgettes and stir-fry for 1–2 minutes.

2 Add the Chinese cabbage, beansprouts and spring onions to the wok. Mix well, then stir-fry the mixture for 1 minute over a high heat.

3 Add the soy sauce, rice wine and sugar. Stir-fry for 30 seconds, then lightly toss in all the noodles and the coriander. Serve the noodles piled on a plate.

Thai Fried Rice

INGREDIENTS

225g/8oz/generous 1 cup Thai jasmine rice
1.5 litres/2½ pints/6 cups boiling water
1 red pepper, seeded
350g/12oz skinless, boneless chicken breasts
45ml/3 tbsp vegetable oil
1 onion, chopped
1 garlic clove, crushed
15ml/1 tbsp mild curry paste
2.5ml/½ tsp paprika
2.5ml/½ tsp ground turmeric
30ml/2 tbsp Thai fish sauce (nam pla)
2 eggs, beaten
salt and ground black pepper
deep fried basil leaves, to garnish

SERVES 4

1 Wash the rice well, drain it and put it in a heavy-based saucepan. Add the boiling water, return to the boil, and then simmer for about 10 minutes, until just tender. Drain well in a colander, then spread out the grains on a baking sheet and leave to cool.

2 Cut the red pepper and the chicken breasts into small cubes. Heat a wok, then add 30ml/ 2 tbsp of the oil and swirl it around. Add the onion and red pepper and stir-fry for 1 minute.

3 Add the chicken, garlic, curry paste and spices and stir-fry for 2–3 minutes.

4 Reduce the heat to medium, add the cooled rice, fish sauce and seasoning. Stir-fry for 2–3 minutes, until the rice is very hot.

5 Make a well in the centre of the rice and add the rest of the oil. When hot, add the beaten eggs, leave to cook for 2 minutes, until the eggs are just  lightly set, then stir them into the rice mixture, using a spatula or a pair of bamboo chopsticks.

6 Scatter over the deep fried basil leaves and serve at once, straight from the wok.

Noodles in Soup

INGREDIENTS

350g/12oz dried egg noodles
600ml/1 pint/2½ cups stock
30ml/2 tbsp vegetable oil
2 spring onions, thinly shredded
225g/8oz chicken breast fillet, pork fillet, or
ready-cooked meat, thinly shredded
115g/4oz/1 cup spinach leaves, lettuce hearts,
or Chinese leaves, thinly shredded
115g/4oz/1 cup drained sliced bamboo
shoots, thinly shredded
3-4 dried shiitake mushrooms, soaked, squeezed
dry and shredded (stalks discarded)
5ml/1 tsp salt
2.5ml/½ tsp soft light brown sugar
15ml/1 tbsp light soy sauce
30ml/2 tsp Chinese rice wine or dry sherry
a few drops sesame oil
chilli sauce, to serve

SERVES 4

1 Cook the noodles in boiling water according to the instructions on the packet, drain, then rinse under cold water. Place in a serving bowl. Bring the stock to the boil, pour over the noodles and keep hot.

2 Heat the oil in a preheated wok, add the spring onions and meat, and stir-fry for about 1 minute.

3 Add the greens, bamboo shoots and mushrooms. Stir-fry for 1 minute, then mix in the salt, sugar, soy sauce, rice wine or sherry and sesame oil. Pour the vegetable

mixture into the serving bowl, on top of the noodles. Serve at once with the chilli sauce.

60

Singapore Noodles

INGREDIENTS

225g/8oz dried egg noodles
45ml/3 tbsp groundnut oil
1 onion, chopped
2.5cm/1in fresh root ginger,
finely chopped
1 garlic clove, finely chopped
15ml/1 tbsp Madras curry powder
2.5ml/½ tsp salt
115g/4oz cooked chicken or pork,
finely shredded
115g/4oz cooked peeled prawns
115g/4oz Chinese cabbage leaves, shredded
115g/4oz/1 cup beansprouts
60ml/4 tbsp chicken stock
15-30ml/1-2 tbsp dark soy sauce
1-2 fresh red chillies, seeded and finely
shredded, to garnish
4 spring onions, finely shredded, to garnish

SERVES 4

61

1 Cook the noodles according to the instructions on the packet. Rinse under cold water and drain well. Toss in 15ml/1 tbsp of the oil and set aside. Heat a wok, add the remaining oil and stir-fry the onion, ginger and garlic for about 2 minutes.

2 Stir the curry powder and salt into the vegetables and stir-fry for 30 seconds, then add the noodles, meat and prawns. Stir-fry for 3–4 minutes.

3 Add the Chinese cabbage and bean-sprouts and stir-fry for 2 minutes. Drizzle the stock and soy sauce over. Toss, then garnish with the chillies and spring onions.

Chinese Jewelled Rice

INGREDIENTS

350g/12oz/1⅔ cups long grain rice
900ml/1½ pints/3¾ cups water
45ml/3 tbsp vegetable oil
1 onion, roughly chopped
115g/4oz/1 cup peas, thawed if frozen
115g/4oz cooked ham, diced
175g/6oz drained canned white crabmeat
75g/3oz/½ cup drained canned water
chestnuts, cut in cubes
4 dried black Chinese mushrooms, soaked,
drained and diced
30ml/2 tbsp oyster sauce
5ml/1 tsp sugar
whole chives, to garnish

SERVES 4

1 Rinse the rice. Bring the water to the boil in a saucepan, add the rice and cover the pan tightly. Cook over a low heat for 12 minutes, then refresh under cold water. Heat the wok, then add half the oil. Stir-fry the rice for 3 minutes, then remove and set aside.

2 Add the remaining oil to the wok. When the oil is hot, add the onion and stir-fry briefly, until it has softened but not coloured.

3 Add the rest of the ingredients and stir-fry for 2 minutes. Return the rice to the wok and stir-fry for 3 minutes more. Serve, garnished with chives.

62

Nutty Rice & Mushroom Stir-fry

INGREDIENTS

350g/12oz/1⅔ cups long grain rice
750-900ml/1¼-1½ pints/
3-3¾ cups water
45ml/3 tbsp sunflower oil
1 small onion, roughly chopped
225g/8oz/2 cups field mushrooms, sliced
50g/2oz/½ cup hazelnuts, roughly chopped
50g/2oz/½ cup pecan nuts, roughly chopped
50g/2oz/½ cup almonds, roughly chopped
60ml/4 tbsp chopped fresh parsley
salt and ground black pepper
parsley sprigs, to garnish

SERVES 4–6

4 Add all the nuts and stir-fry for 1 minute. Add the rice to the wok and stir-fry for about 3 minutes. Season. Stir in the parsley. Garnish with parsley sprigs and serve.

1 Rinse the rice. Bring the water to the boil in a saucepan with a tight-fitting lid. Add the rice, cover and cook for 10–12 minutes. When it is cooked, refresh under cold water. Heat the wok, then add half the oil. When the oil is hot, stir-fry the rice for 2–3 minutes. Remove and set aside.

2 Add the remaining oil to the wok and stir-fry the onion for 2 minutes until softened.

3 Mix in the field mushrooms and stir-fry for 2 minutes over a high heat.

63

Index